"This book is intense—in a really, really great way. There are full-on teachings on character and identity, and fervent calls towards excellence and creativity. Anthony Skinner has a fire in his heart to worship God, and to encourage and equip others to do the same. The intensity of that passion burns though every chapter of this really helpful book."

—Matt Redman

"*WORSHIP SMARTbook: Actionable Tips for Real-World Worship* is a necessary guide for every worship leader! Anthony takes a very refreshing and simplistic approach to answering the questions every worship leader asks. This book is not only an invaluable resource, but every detail is made fully accessible no matter where you are in your experience with worship leading. I strongly recommend this book for every worship leader, pastor, and musician who desires to grow in their worship. *WORSHIP SMARTbook: Actionable Tips for Real-World Worship* will take you and your team to a new level of excellence!"

—Kim Walker-Smith, Jesus Culture

2012 Editors Pick, for the "Best of the Best Issue" in *Worship Leader* magazine.

—*Worship Leader* magazine

"Anthony Skinner is one of the most truly creative individuals I've ever met. His music is a refreshing banquet that continually surprises me. And now he provides us with insights into another aspect of his gifting: wisdom. *Actionable Tips for Real-World Worship* is a practical handbook on worship and worship leading. Whether it's troubleshooting for problem issues, staying connected to God, leading people in worship, or leading a band, this book offers insights that could cut years of guesswork for novice and veteran worship leader alike. Anthony also dives deeply into the real heart of the issue: ushering people into the presence of God. This book is an invaluable tool for anyone wanting to grow in excellence in the privileged role of leading in worship."

—Bill Johnson, Bethel Church, and
author of *When Heaven Invades Earth* and *Dreaming with God*

"From a leader of worship leaders, Anthony Skinner has distilled his breadth of experience into a very practical guide for anyone who participates in or supports modern church worship music. There is something in here for everyone, delivered in easy to find bite-sized morsels and with Anthony's customary passion for God and heart of care for people. This is a worthy resource for anyone wanting to develop or support worship music ministry."

—Casey McGinty, Senior Vice President, EMI CMG Publishing

"Anthony Skinner is the real deal: an artist whose lyrics stimulate and innovate, a worship leader whose love for the Lord overflows in a lifestyle of mercy and justice. I commend him and this book wholeheartedly."

—Pete Greig, 24-7 Prayer and Alpha International

"This generation needs dreamers. For far too long the church has been imitating and following instead of leading. Anthony Skinner is breathing creative life in such a desolate landscape. His insight, leadership, and creativity is fierce roar. Eat up these words and begin to dream again. May your church become a river of transformation in your city."

—Daniel Bashta

"Anthony Skinner is one of my favorite singer/songwriters and worship leaders. There is a rare depth to him, and I believe any person could benefit greatly from the wealth of his experiences, especially in the worship community."

—John Mark McMillan

"I know Anthony as a friend, brother, and fellow worshiper. His heart and gifting has caused me to encounter Jesus in deeply intimate ways. Prepare yourself for the same as you experience the insights of this great project."

—Steve Berger, founding pastor, Grace Chapel

# WORSHIP
# SMARTbook

## ACTIONABLE TIPS FOR
## REAL-WORLD WORSHIP

### by
### Anthony Skinner

**Out of the Cave Music**
**Franklin, Tennessee**

Published by:
Out of the Cave Music and
Orphansake Records
Franklin, TN 37064
www.anthonyskinner.com
contact@anthonyskinner.com

# Dedication

This book is dedicated to those who are taking the creative risk to pull what is unseen and unheard into the realm of the seen and heard, and to those who are taking the time to develop and craft that something into a song, a moment, and a message that gives glory to God and encouragement, strength, comfort, and healing to others.

# Thank You

To Mary Keith Skinner, for your encouragement, feedback, and insight; to Angelo Ballestero and Bryan Lenox, for your friendship and support; and to Ivan Pato and Janis Whipple, for your contribution to this book.

# WORSHIP SMARTbook:
# Actionable Tips for Real-World Worship
# Table of Contents

Sing joyfully to the LORD, you righteous;
it is fitting for the upright to praise him.
Praise the LORD with the harp;
make music to him on the ten-stringed lyre.
Sing to him a new song;
play skillfully, and shout for joy.
For the word of the LORD is right and true;
he is faithful in all he does.
The LORD loves righteousness and justice;
the earth is full of his unfailing love.

—Psalm 33:1–5

# Introduction

One of the few things we will continue to do from now through eternity is worship. We will be worshiping God for His beauty, love, salvation, majesty, and mystery forever. As one involved in every aspect of worship—from writing songs to leading worship to producing worship music—I am always humbled to be part of this eternal and everlasting process. Whatever your relationship is to worship, you also are investing in one of the most foolproof of opportunities when you engage in your God-given part of the process. Besides worship giving God the honor He is due, the Bible states clearly that worship wins battles, sends demonic oppression fleeing, conveys courage and truth to listeners, brings strategy to problems, and actually results in the inhabitation of God! Wow!

With all of these benefits to worship, it has been a real yearning of mine for years to write a book to help both the novice and the professional get the most out of their time leading worship. Think about it . . . if our big payoff in eternity is to worship God face-to-face, then worship on earth should have an excellence that births yearning, hunger, new life, and revelation of the beauty of God and His worth to believers *and* unbelievers. Worship should be the ultimate experience. This sort of a calling to excellence is paved with a relationship to God, lots of prayer, and hard work.

In this book, I have taken tips discovered through my own mistakes and victories as well as those passed along through relationship with other worshipers. My desire is that my ceiling, and that of many of my fellow worship leaders, would be your floor. I pray that your excellence would skyrocket, so the knowledge of God would cover the earth like the waters cover the sea.

Behind the worship experience, there are so many people with different wirings and skills involved. It has also been in my heart to help bridge the gap of communication between all the different "participants" in worship—from the pastor and the worship leader; to the drummer, the guitarist, and the sound guy; to the mixed media person and the worship team; to the "creatives" and the administrator. My desire is that this book would help build better communication and understanding within the extended worship team.

## How to Use this Book

If you are a worship leader, consider going through the chapters as a team . . . one smart chapter per week. Use the information and layout of this book as a team-building tool.

If you are a pastor or administrator, read the book through and pray for ways you can support your worship team or help them serve you better. Then share it with others on the team and pray for more understanding, love, and unity to build with all the different people involved.

If you are a player, you can use the book to strengthen your personal skill level and

# INTRODUCTION

better understand how to fit into a band or worship team setting, as well as learn practical ways to serve your worship leader and the bigger vision.

If you are a support team member, this book can give valuable insight into ways you can build up the team and provide a better worship experience for your church.

Personalize the book for your team or your experience. Don't be afraid to add other points. Music is personal—every player, every church is unique. Each comes with its own set of strengths and weaknesses, so use this resource in the way that works best for you.

Peace and love,

Anthony

# Leadership

Music is your own experience, your thoughts, your wisdom. If you don't live it, it won't come out of your horn.

—Charlie Parker

# Smart Chapter #1
# Bulletproof!

*(Finding Your Identity Is Simpler Than You Think)*

## 1. Identity is crucial to leadership.

This is a simple principle, but it must be fleshed out each day. Leaders who know their identity are safer to follow than someone who is trying to prove something.

## 2. God wants us to derive our primary identity from spiritual truth.

Our primary identity is our spiritual identity (meaning what we look like to God . . . or *perceive* we look like to God). Everything else about our self-identity must be built on this foundation. We are loved by God and therefore we love God back. We are beautiful because that is how God sees us. Period. That simple! In all reality, *this* is what a worship leader's call is: to be an example of those who know how to receive the love of God and how to lavish God with our loving response to His love. A worship leader should know how to enjoy being seen as beautiful by God . . . blemishes and all!

## 3. We are typically bent on deriving our identity from what we do.

Most people define their lives by their skills, looks, relationships, gift sets, place in the company, ministry, latest song they've written, etc. If those things are favorable, then they feel successful. If such factors are not favorable, then people feel unsuccessful. This type of thinking is built on a lie and sets up a person for major disappointment. It also hinders a worship leader from truly imparting an accurate picture of the freedom that comes through the love of God. Nothing is wrong with drawing your purpose, identity, and satisfaction from what you do. As a matter of fact, you can't escape it. Just make sure all of it builds on and follows your spiritual identity—what God says about you.

**Hot Tip!**

**The Lord knew that King David would never be a safe king and leader until his identity was in the Lord and not in what he did. The same is true for you!**

### 4. Satan wants to define us by our sin and our shortcomings.

How often do you think of yourself in the light of what you haven't done or what you've just done wrong? Be careful or "I can't sing" becomes "I'm not a singer," or "I feel ugly" becomes "I am ugly," or "I can't play guitar" becomes "I am not a guitar player," or "that sin is ugly in me" becomes "I am ugly to God." Let the love of God define you. Allow Him to love you and then love Him right back. Say yes to God's definition of you—daily and even hourly!

*Fact*: You are successful in the most dynamic sense of the word, because God loves you and created you for a love relationship with Him, and you said yes to His love. That decision turned you from a pauper to a prince . . . in an instant. That makes you one of the most successful people in history. You are one of God's success stories for all eternity!

*Fact*: God has made us to find satisfaction and significance in the things we do. These things are important, and we will always find some identity in these things! Yet God just wants them to be secondary to His love for us in defining us.

## Smart Chapter #1
# Bulletproof!
### *Discussion Questions*

1. Would you say that you mostly regret the past, fear the future, or live in the present?

2. How do you think God sees you?  Do you think He's mostly happy with you or mostly disappointed with you?

3. On a practical daily basis, do you primarily define yourself by:
a.  The truth that God loves you and chose you just as you are?
b.  All the good things you do?
c.  Your shortcomings?

Remember, we have to be good receivers before we can be good givers. The better we are at being loved *by* God, the better lovers *of* God we'll be. A key to growing in love and passion toward Him is learning to practice awareness of *His* passionate love for *you* on a daily basis.

**Hot Tip!**

**Make it a point every day to give new value or weight to the truth that God's love for you far outweighs any good or bad thing you could ever do.**

## Smart Chapter #2
# Keeping the Fire Stoked

Lukewarm or cold . . . neither are an option for any Christian, and there's definitely no place for them in a worshiper's life.

"I know your deeds, that you are neither cold nor hot. I wish you were either one or the other! So, because you are lukewarm—neither hot nor cold—I am about to spit you out of my mouth" (Revelation 3:15–16). Yikes, no one ever wants to have this said about them. Truth is, most anything that is lukewarm is a turnoff. Have you ever enjoyed a song when the singer had no passion? Ever read a book where the author was casual about his subject? Have you ever been in a relationship when someone had lukewarm feelings about you? Ouch. God is no different. The truth is, we give attention to the things we care about. "You and I do those things that we care about. There are things in your life that get done because you care about them. There are other things that don't get done. Why? Because you don't care as much about them."[1]

### 1. Stay in the Word.

What books of the Bible are you currently reading? What commentaries do you own? What scriptures are your favorites? Who are your favorite Bible teachers? Be a worshiper who can enthusiastically answer these questions.

### 2. Experience the joy of prayer.

Our goal in life is to "keep our hearts in front of the fire of God's love."[2] Constant prayer is one way to do this. As Paul says, we are to "Pray without ceasing" (1 Thessalonians 5:17, NKJV). Charles Spurgeon wrote, "Prayer gives a channel to the pent-up sorrows of the soul, they flow away, and in their stead streams of sacred delight pour into the heart. At the same time the more rejoicing the more praying; when the heart is in a quiet condition, and full of joy in the Lord, then also will it be sure to draw nigh unto the Lord in worship. Holy joy and prayer act and react upon each other. . . . These three precepts are an ornament of grace to every believer's neck, wear them every one of you, for glory and for beauty; 'Rejoice evermore;' 'Pray without ceasing;' 'In everything give thanks.'"[3]

### 3. Be consistent.

Don't let your attitude and your faith be different onstage and off. There should be no difference in the attitude and thoughts of your heart and mind whether you are leading worship onstage or living your daily life offstage.

### 4. Develop and maintain healthy boundaries.

Jesus had His twelve and His three, and still constantly pulled away to have alone time with God. Establish healthy habits and boundaries in your life. You need those two or three friends who have your back, but you have to have time for you, and time for you and God.

### 5. Establish an attitude of gratitude.

You are getting paid (in portion) to pursue your passions. Always remember you would be pursuing God and music regardless of the pay. Avoid falling into the trap of Christianity becoming your job. You must keep your passions out in front of your paycheck. Practically speaking, don't study and prepare just because you have a service to do; do it because you care.

### 6. Retreat!

Schedule times throughout the year to take a personal retreat. This doesn't have to be expensive. Anything that allows you to pull away from life's distractions and listen to God will do. Spend a night at a nearby hotel, take a trip to a cabin, go camping out in nature. Whatever allows you to unplug from the business and plug deeper into God.

**Hot Tip!**

**Maturity and consistency is more about a "want to" than a "how to." If you want to, then you'll figure out how to be faithful and mature. If you don't "want to," then "how to" doesn't really matter.**

**Smart Chapter #2**
# Keeping the Fire Stoked
*Discussion Questions*

1. What time of day do you most enjoy reading Scripture?

2. With regard to reading Scripture, what steps can you take to set yourself up to succeed?

3. A practicle step toward maintaining an attitude of gratitude is to daily make a list of the top ten things you are currently thankful for.  Can you list ten things today that you are thankful for?

1.

2.

3.

4.

5.

6.

7.

8.

9.

10.

Remember to look at the next calendar year and determine now when you can take a personal retreat/or retreats.

# Smart Chapter #3
# You and Your Pastor
### *(Pastors, Elders, and Leadership)*

Learning to connect with and serve your pastor and the leadership can be the difference in either looking forward to the beginning or the end of the day.

## 1. Stay connected.

Stay connected to your pastor and leadership. If you're not intentional, you may only see your pastor during church and staff meetings. You've got to make time to get together outside of the office. Seek ways to occasionally laugh and blow off steam together.

## 2. Serve the sermon.

Make sure you are on the same page with whoever is preaching or teaching on the weekend. Connect a week or so ahead. This will help you decide on directions, songs, and attitude of your worship time. Of course there are exceptions, and at times things will take a directional change, but you can powerfully serve God and your pastor by preparing ahead.

## 3. Write your pastor a letter.

Letter writing is a lost art, but it's still a great way to let someone know you care. As you might already know, the role of a pastor can be a thankless job. Say thank you or "Thinking about you" in a handwritten letter. No reason to be lengthy—a simple encouraging word and/or a scripture verse can go a long way.

## 4. Remember birthdays.

He's the guy who always has to remember everybody else. Make sure you remember your pastor's birthday!

## Hot Tip!

**Think of your pastor and elders as extended family, rather than just coworkers. Take the time to build strong healthy re-lationships. Learn to talk through concerns and feel-ings while respecting one another's boundaries.**

## 5. Serve outside of the church setting.

Don't get locked into only serving one way, through the music. Get your hands dirty. Help your pastor or one of the elders with some yard work. Do an outreach to the poor together. If you find ways to connect and serve outside your normal setting, chances are you'll find out something new about God and each other. God has a way of empowering you through these types of situations, and you can then take these discoveries back into your normal ministry setting.

## Smart Chapter #3
# You and Your Pastor
*Discussion Questions*

1. Can you list five birthdays of people with whom you work?
   1.
   2.
   3.
   4.
   5.

2. Add the five birthdays (listed above) to your calendar. Go ahead and buy birthday cards for each person on the list. Lastly, put each card in a properly addressed, stamped envelope so you will be ready to write in/sign the card, and send it off at the appropriate time.

## Smart Chapter #4
# Establishing a Culture of Honor

**Honor**, n. on'or. [L. honor, honos.] The esteem due or paid to worth; high estimation.

As a leader and/or team/band member you must establish a culture of honor. This is done through your actions as well as your words.

## 1. Let it begin with you.

Leader or not, people are always watching you. Treat your pastor, leadership, church members, and band with honor. If you talk about others in a negative light, your team will follow suit. Conversely, if you exhibit honor toward others, your team will learn to do the same.

## 2. Seek clarity.

Look people in the eye, be clear and honest in your communication, and be straightforward with your expectations.

## 3. Maintain an effective supply line.

Get people the information they need so they have adequate time to prepare for what's expected.

## 4. Return phone calls.

We've all been guilty of dropping the ball here. Make it a priority to return phone calls  (also text messages and emails) as soon as possible. Don't leave your team hanging.

## 5. Include your sound person.

Make the sound person a part of your team, a part of the band. This person is your lifeline to the people and that's super-important. Honor them!

**Hot Tip!**

**The music will always be stronger when everyone is on the same page and headed in the same direction.**

### 6. Honor each other.

You can do this by being punctual and prepared. You can also do this by remaining patient and focused during practice. Stay attentive rather than having to be called to attention.

### 7. Be clear and purposeful.

You can further establish a culture of honor by being clear and purposeful about serving the big picture, the vision, of your leadership and church. Keeping this in focus will help eliminate little personal agendas that might pop up from time to time.

## Smart Chapter #4
# Establishing a Culture of Honor
*Discussion Questions*

1. Make an easily accessible "to do" list on your phone or computer. Keep a running list of people you need to contact/return phone calls, etc. Reference the list once a week and keep it updated.

2. What can you do to ensure that you are outwardly and purposefully expressing your gratitude to those on your team?

**Smart Chapter #5**
# How to Encourage while Leading, Guiding, and Correcting

The point of this smart chapter is to assist you in being authentic with your encouragement. We tend to focus on the negative too often. It's hard to only hear instruction or correction without affirmation. God doesn't do this to us, so let's not do it to each other—especially in the creative arts, where there is so much risk and vulnerability related to putting your ideas and your heart on the table. Try these simple sentences. This may sound silly, but it really does work. Say them out loud, work on them, make them your own, and remember to always affirm your team members when steering the ship.

## 1. To the entire team:

*"You guys sound great! I love the way this song is coming together."*

## 2. To single out a particular player for affirmation:

For example, to (John Doe) on drums: *"John, that was great the way you brought it down and then exploded into the chorus."*

## 3. To an individual player who needs some correction mixed with affirmation:

Let's say you have a guitar player who is typically a "busy" player (tendency to overplay). You could say, *"Can you create some space for the vocals here?"* or *"I love the way the guitars are creating space for the vocals on this part."* This makes it about the vocals and not the guitars, but you are still being an encourager.

## 4. To your sound person during rehearsal:

*"Can you give me some more of that kick in my monitor? I gotta have more of my man (John Doe) on the drums!"* This affirms your player

**Hot Tip!**

**Make sure you acknowledge your team/ band members after they have gotten something right or when they are excelling. You don't want to only encourage while "trying to get there." Encourage and celebrate your players all the way through the process.**

and lets the sound person know what you need and the importance of his or her part on the team.

### 5. To encourage your team/band members to be creative:

*"That was great! I really liked that one part in particular on the verse section. I was thinking, what about trying this idea on the chorus? What do you think?"* Giving creative license is a great way to pull gold out of people. Just make sure you are giving more to those who can handle it and less to those who can't.

### 6. To a player with a solo, encouragement plus suggestion:

*"I loved that solo man, you nailed it! Can you come down just a bit and still play the solo just like you did it that time? I loved it, loved the way you . . ."* Take a moment to share the parts that really got you going.

### 7. Another way to affirm and correct:

*"I love your energy on that part! I wonder if we can keep the energy, but turn it down a little bit?"*

### 8. Suggestion for encouraging while asking for change in volume:

Let's say your guitar player is playing too loudly. You could say, *"I love the intensity. I wonder if we could turn down the overall volume of the band, and maybe we should bring the guitars back a little more than everyone else, but let's not lose that intensity. I love it . . . and wanna keep it!"*

**Smart Chapter #5**
# How to Encourage while Leading, Guiding, and Correcting
*Discussion Questions*

1. How do you normally talk to your band/team?  Write down a phrase you might normally use when trying to guide and lead.

2. Now write down some of the phrases from this chapter in your own words and commit to using them for positive reinforcement this week.

3. List the different people in your band/team by name. Now write out some specific language, phrases that you can use to encourage, build up, guide, and direct them.

**Smart Chapter #6**
# The Worship Leader's Law of Averages: 15/15/70 Rule!

## 1. Fifteen percent of people will go with you . . . anywhere, anytime.

Yes, 15 percent of your congregation is always enthusiastic, ready, and willing to follow your leadership regardless of how good, prepared, or qualified you are.

## 2. Fifteen percent will typically stay where they are.

Let's face it, there are always people who would rather be somewhere else, regardless of whether it's church or not! These people can be pretty resistant to your leadership, and will usually check out early. (*It's not personal*, at least not most of the time.)

## 3. Seventy percent are up for grabs and want a leader.

That's right, *the bulk* of the congregation is usually open and willing to engage, but *they need you to lead them* on the journey. You have a window of time with these people, so you have to maximize it.

## 4. Guess what? You can be that leader!

If you've been given the position of leadership at this time, then you are the man or woman for the job. Don't waste time second-guessing yourself—no one has it all together. Instead, take the reins, apply this 15/15/70 rule, and use it to help you identify where people are so you can bring them along. People want a shepherd.

## Hot Tip!

**Get your direction from God, check in with your pastor, and then be open to where the people are, so you can meet them there.**

### 5. Be active, vocal, and purposeful with your encouragement.

Pastor your people. *Be appreciative of the supportive worshipers, engage them, and make eye contact.* Then pastor the 70 percent that are learning a lifestyle of worship. Encourage them as you worship, bring them into the moment, and give small exhortations and explanations if the Spirit starts to move (example: Peter in Acts 2). You will automatically get your supportive 15 percent and gain a higher percentage of the rest of the congregation as well. That typically resistant 15 percent might even warm up and come along before you know it!

*Special Note*: Don't be discouraged with the 15 percent group that won't come along or get lazy with the 15 percent group that *always* comes along and forget about those other guys, the 70 percent! Give everyone their due weight and allow God to sharpen your skills of communication, compassion, and humor as you lead the 15/15/70.

### Hot Tip! (the Seesaw)

As worship leaders, most of us tend to focus on either the 15 percent who love to worship, because they make us feel good as leaders, or on the 15 percent that won't engage and send off an intimidating vibe. *Don't base what you are doing on either group.* It's impossible to please all people, but it is very possible to please God.

**Smart Chapter #6**
# The Worship Leader's
# Law of Averages: 15/15/70 Rule!
*Discussion Questions*

1. Based on chapter #6, what 15 percent do you normally find yourself focusing on?

2. Is it easy for you to get down on yourself because of the 15 percent that don't go with you so easily?

3. Do you see the 70 percent as an opportunity or a daunting task, and why?

4. What steps can you take to engage the 70 percent and encourage them to worship?

Ask God if there is any rejection or place of hurt that has left you especially vulnerable to the opinions of others. How did He see you in that moment of feeling misunderstood? Let Him love on you and tell you how beautiful you are!

## Smart Chapter #7
# Praying before a Service or Worship Time

### 1. Why pray beforehand?

Let's be honest, it's easy to lose your reason "why," especially when you are busy with the technicalities of pulling off a worship service. The worship leader's world can consist of early mornings, frustrating sound checks, and long rehearsals. Remember, your band/worship team members come to the service time with many things competing for their attention. Bringing them together as a group before you have to lead others in worship can be a powerful tool to provide focus and help everyone remember *why* they are there. Make sure you make time for this crucial time of prayer.

### 2. When should you pray?

Don't wait until someone says it's time to start the music. Make this time an intentional part of your preparation, and make sure to take enough time (fifteen to twenty minutes) for everyone to center themselves through prayer. The last thing you want is to run on stage feeling rushed.

### 3. Where should you pray?

If possible, find a quite corner or room where you can hear others and you don't have to pray loudly to be heard.

### 4. Pray for God's promises and people's needs!

These are two great things for us to rally around in prayer time. Ask if anyone has a need and cover it with love, then declare God's promises.

**Hot Tip!**

**Check out Psalm 136. It's a great form to follow from time to time when praying in a group. Try having one person lead and others answer or echo (i.e. "Give thanks to the Lord, for he is good." "His love endures forever." "Give thanks to the God of gods." "His love endures forever" [Psalm 136:1–2]).**

## 5. Circle up!

You don't always have to circle up and pray, but grabbing a hand is great for unity!

## 6. Keep it brief.

The point of this time is to come together, not to hear someone's life history. If someone gets long-winded, lovingly and respectfully pull the focus back to the moment at hand. If something requires more attention, personally commit to listening to the need after the service (then make sure you don't forget)!

## 7. Seek quiet.

Take a minute for everyone to quiet down their spirits and listen to God. In the quiet, someone might get an impression, unction, thought, or "word" that gives some important last-minute guidance to your worship time. Also, share with your team any impressions you have already received about what God would like to do through the worship time. It helps build unity, excitement, and focus as a band to share these thoughts with your battling buddies!

## 8. Pray over your team.

Pray for your team. They are absolutely instrumental to the task, so treat them as such. Ask God to bless their thoughts, hearts, voices, and hands as they sing and play, and their hands and feet as they drum. At this point, you have done all you can do to be prepared (you've prepared your heart, practiced, rehearsed, had your sound check) and now it is time to declare your dependency on God to add His anointing to your humble offering. End by thanking God for His goodness. An attitude of gratitude is infectious and ending your prayer time with a focus on His goodness will carry over in faith as you pick up your instruments and lead your congregation!

### Smart Chapter #7
# Praying before a Service or Worship Time
*Discussion Questions*

1. Do you regularly pray before your service or worship time?


2. Do you take the time to pray over/for your band/team members before service time?


3. Does your prayer time feel authentic?


4. What steps can you take to make it a more meaningful moment?

## Smart Chapter #8
# Making an Emotional Connection

Connecting yourself and your team to the meanings behind the songs will help your audience have a connection to the songs as well. Your goal is for everyone in your audience to have one or more connection points within a song or set of songs. If you haven't lived that connection to the music and lyrics you're leading, you cannot effectively invite your audience to connect emotionally either.

## 1. You want to create moments that people can take away with them.

People are looking for a real experience. The key here is, people are already looking. So with that in mind, what is in your life . . . in the songs you choose . . . in the players you use . . . that can be a part of supplying this experience to your audience or congregation?

## 2. Remember, people key off of you.

Have you experienced the song you are playing yet? By that I mean, does it speak to your heart, soul, and spirit? Does it capture, touch, or impact you? If you aren't impacted by a song, chances are your audience won't be either.

## 3. Dive deeper into your song.

If you have been impacted by a song and *can* figure out why, then you are one step further to knowing how to give that song away. Write down what the song does and/or is doing for and to you.

## 4. Develop a compass for creating moments within the song.

Use #3 above as a guideline to find and develop live moments in each song. If a particular section of a song is special, then don't be in a hurry to blow past it; instead, camp out there for a minute, play the line again, emphasis it, or come back around to it at the end of the song.

**Hot Tip!**

**You want to translate a genuine experience. This all starts by being genuine. Ask God to help you get comfortable in your own skin. Discover your identity and confidence in Christ. It's a beautiful thing to stand before others and not need their adulation. It frees you up to be focused on giving and not getting.**

### 5. Stay with what's working.

In football, if a team is scoring double digits, the idea is to stick with what's working. If you try something during a song and it works great, it will probably work great again. Make a mental note of what's worked in the past, but don't be a one-trick pony. Always look for and be prepared to find other ways to make a song special.

### 6. Leadership is 24–7.

Your week, your practice, your rehearsal, the choices you make, the way you treat others—all of this helps create momentum leading up to your delivery onstage. God may likely be giving you guidance on your theme, prayer direction, song choice, etc. throughout the week leading up to your time onstage.

### 7. Take some of the same cues above and apply them to the stage.

"If songs look the same, they start sounding the same. Communication is 15 percent the words, 30 percent how passionate they are, and 55 percent what the audience sees with their eyes. . . . The idea is to be just as creative in communication as you are musically."[4]

## Smart Chapter #8
# Making an Emotional Connection
### *Discussion Questions*

1. If 15 percent is the words, 30 percent is how passionate they are, and 55 percent is what the audience sees with their eyes, where does that leave you?

2. What can you do to reinforce what you are saying and singing?

3. What's your current favorite song? Why?

4. Have you ever repeated a phrase or line from a verse or chorus? Could you see yourself doing this? What song could you do this with in a corporate setting?

5. Have you ever practiced repeating a phrase from a verse or chorus during rehearsal?

6. Try taking a phrase that is meaningful in the song and personalizing it in your own words. Consider singing this if it feels good.

**Smart Chapter #9**
# Incoming, Need Prayer!
*(How to Get Started with Prayer Support)*

## 1. You want to be consistent.

Make sure you have strong, stable, and continual prayer support for your worship team/band.

## 2. What if you're feeling the resistance?

If a thriving culture of worship and praise, supported by prayer, provides focus and fuel to a church, then you can bet it is going to be resisted by the enemy. You are in a battle and you need to treat it like one. Strong prayer support is your weapon.

## 3. You need a goal.

Write out a clear goal of why you need a prayer team and what you hope to accomplish with this team. Keep it simple. It doesn't need to be complicated.

## 4. You need a list of band needs.

Set aside some time to talk with your worship team and lay out the vision for a prayer team. Find out the needs of your worship team/band members and write them down.

## 5. You need a list of potential recruits.

Start with asking the people you trust and feel safe with (the easy ones)! Ask those who are natural intercessors, exuberant worshipers, or just close friends who always have time to lift you up.

**Hot Tip!**

**Some people love to pray, just like you love to play an instrument! Do not feel like you are burdening your prayer team members when this just may be what they were created for. And you may walk away with deep friendships for life!**

### 6. A great fit—a worshiper who isn't musical.

Being on your prayer team is a great opportunity for someone who does not have musical talent but wants to be involved in worship.

### 7. Make an announcement at church.

Ask your pastor for a short window during your church service and let people know you are starting a prayer team to support you and the worship team at your church. Be sure to keep your announcement focused and energized and let the people know how they can plug in or who to contact.

### 8. Print it in the bulletin and/or on the website.

Write up a short blurb in your church bulletin and/or on the church's website, letting people know what you are doing. Be sure to list a contact person with a number, email address, or form they can fill out. Make joining the prayer team fun and accessible.

### 9. Establish the prayer point person.

Find a point person to administrate and set up an email system for you, if that is not a strength for you. This will be invaluable, especially for seasons when things are really going berserk. Also, determine who will lead your prayer team. These will not necessarily be the same person.

### 10. Contact those who are interested and set up a meeting.

Make contact with new prayer team volunteers in a timely fashion. At the initial meeting, open with prayer, lay out your vision, present the plan for how communication will take place, take people's input, share the needs of the worship team, and then take time to pray for each other and ask God to bless what you are doing. Try to keep everything, including any fellowship time, within two hours.

## Smart Chapter #9
# Incoming, Need Prayer!
### *Discussion Questions*

1. Do you currently have a prayer team in your church?

2. Do you have someone or a group who prays for you and your worship team? If so, how are you keeping them updated?

3. Can you think of a way to bless that person this week?

4. If you do not have someone who is praying for you and your team, can you think of one to three people who might be interested and contact them?

## Smart Chapter #10
# Nine Ways to Get Your Congregation to Sing

## 1. No more than one, or at most two, of the songs in your worship service should be new to the congregation (in most cases).

With new or old songs, be sure to hit the chorus a number of times. People need a point in the music where their mouths can go on cruise control because they know or can easily pick up the words. Then they can use their energy to get spiritually focused.

## 2. A great way to introduce a new worship song is to play it on a CD before or after a service for a few weeks prior to leading it.

Take this approach for a few weeks and see which songs catch on. Doing this just might give you an idea if a song is a good fit for your people or not.

## 3. Avoid breaks in the music. People tend to warm up to singing as they go, and frequent breaks will leave them cold.

Especially avoid breaks for long sermonettes by the worship leader. Try to let the music flow nicely from one song to the next.

## 4. You typically need to start with upbeat songs. It's hard to go backward.

As a worship leader, you can face unique hurdles. Sometimes people are still waking up, while others may have just finished a heated argument on the way to church. Help get the crowd's blood flowing with upbeat songs, and avoid minor or moody keys to begin with.

**Hot Tip!**

**Part of your enthusiasm should include smiling. It's easy to get so focused and "try so hard" that you forget to smile. So smile!**

## 5. Make eye contact. You must establish that you are a facilitator of worship, not a star performer.

If you have a small group, try to establish eye contact with your congregation and gain their response and support before starting on the worship. This helps prevent you from drifting off into your own world and leaving the rest behind.

## 6. Be enthusiastic. This goes for every visible person "up front."

If there is a pastor or Scripture reader up front while the music is playing, they need to be worshiping as well. The spirit of worship is contagious. You lead with your countenance as well as with what you say and sing.

## 7. Give subtle hints to your congregation to join in worship.

A simple "Let's join in" or "Let's sing together" or even a simple hand motion can go a long way. Sometimes all it takes is asking.

## 8. Avoid scolding. It's easy to get frustrated, but be careful not to mention a congregation's unresponsiveness.

If they're just not responding, don't get discouraged but just keep worshiping while searching for a better connection. Scolding will only result in less participation. You have to earn their participation. Also, sometimes giving them a paradigm like a sports match or a memory of falling in love will help them connect with their more "enthusiastic" self.

## 9. Put them at ease.

Regardless of how responsive your congregation is, many people need permission for a break. You may want to offer them the opportunity to sit after two or three songs of standing. This is especially true if they are new to worship or are older. Your invitation may be as simple as saying, "Please feel free to sit during worship, if you feel more comfortable." Ultimately, you are trying to give them the freedom to experience God in a manner that is not distracting to them.

## Smart Chapter #10
# Nine Ways to Get Your Congregation to Sing
### *Discussion Questions*

1. How comfortable are you with encouraging your congregation to sing along with you?

2. Do you smile when you are leading worship?

3. Do you feel that God or people will only be pleased if you reach a certain spiritual or emotional "plateau" in worship?

4. Have you ever been guilty of driving your congregation to hard to accomplish this?

Remember that success can look a lot of different ways.  God's design can look different each week.  Stay sensitive and check your own motivation.

## Smart Chapter #11
# Communication

Communication works for those who work at it.

—John Powell

## 1. Choose the right song.

If you choose a song you can identify with, it will be much easier for people to identify with the song as well.

## 2. Overcome shyness.

One of the hardest things to overcome as a musician or worship leader is stage fright. A great way to conquer this fear is to remember that you are playing for Jesus and you already have His approval! Imagine He is sitting on the front row, cheering for you and enjoying you. You were created to worship Him. Perfect love truly casts out fear. Focus on Him—His great love for you, His approval of you—and soon you will not be able to hide your response.

## 3. Use dynamics to communicate a song.

Many familiar worship choruses are simple and consist of three to four chords played over and over. Using dynamics—becoming louder in certain places and softer in others—will help capture your audience's attention and point their hearts toward God. However, make sure your dynamic choices make sense within the context of the song. (See smart chapter #29 on Dynamics for more suggestions.)

## 4. Use body language to communicate.

Never stand or play as if you were bored of a song—or worship leading in general. Stay engaged, grateful, and on point. People will notice when you are sincere and passionate. They will also know when you are not. Learn to "listen" to how a song is affecting you as you lead. If a song is actually boring you or doesn't seem to have the "juice" on it for some reason, the Holy Spirit may be letting you know He would rather work through a different song. Learn to read how a song ministers to yourself as well as your audience, and learn to make the transition to something more effective if the Spirit changes things up a bit.

### 5. Play each song like it's the first time!

Even if you're leading a song everyone knows, play it like it's the first time anyone has ever heard it. Truth never grows old . . . and neither does a good melody!

### 6. Play skillfully. Always use tasteful licks while performing.

Do not run over the singers with busy guitar licks, drum accents, and bad choices of effects. There will be appropriate places for you to do your thing. Be patient while the vocals pass the message on to the crowd. Then use your moment to enhance the song.

### 7. Acknowledge your audience.

Make sure not to ignore your audience when you are ministering in song. Acknowledge and address them. You can introduce yourself and introduce your song as well. Occasionally express why the song means so much to you, but be sure to keep it brief. Let the song be the agent of ministry, not your personal commentary.

### 8. Make eye contact.

Don't be afraid to make eye contact with your audience. It makes them feel a part of the song and engages them in the worship experience as a whole.

### 9. Be yourself! Be confident about who you are in Christ and let your light shine.

Don't overthink what you do, say, and play. Enjoy yourself!

## Smart Chapter #11
# Communication
*Discussion Questions*

1. Do you struggle with fear?

2. Have you struggled with rejection?

3. Is there someone you know that supports what you are doing that you can talk to?

4. Do you struggle with being succinct?

**Hot Tip!**

**We all need a David and Jonathan relationship that we can go to.**

**Hot Tip!**

**Play each song like it's the first time it's ever been heard.**

5. If you do struggle with being succinct, take some time to write down what a song means to you or why you are choosing this week's songs. Keep working on it until you get it down to a few simple phrases, then you can use these phrases during your worship service.

Pick a few songs you are currently using, and take the next two pages to complete this excercise.

Remember to play each song like it's the first time!  Sometimes it helps to approach  an old song with new instrumentation  (i.e. if an upbeat song has really  great meaty lyrics, maybe you can slow it down and do it acoustically  with only a few instruments).  Allow people a moment to ponder the  power of the lyric by singing it slowly. Then, let your drummer count off a fast tempo and kick into it.

# Smart Chapter #12
# Your Sound Team:
# A Solid Plan + Patience = Success

You can prepare all you want, rehearse, practice, buy the best gear—but at the end of the day, what your sound person knows and hears will directly translate into what your audience will hear. The rub is that in most church settings, the sound person is typically a volunteer. This requires you to have a solid plan and great patience. Here are a few tips to help you choose and work with your sound team.

## 1. Have a plan.

Get a plan together. Be wise when choosing your team to run sound. Write down a job description. If applicable, create a form that interested people can fill out. If you are not clear about what you want, you'll never be certain about what you get.

## 2. Maintain an attitude of gratitude.

Go into this process with an attitude of gratitude. Be appreciative of the fact that you have someone who wants to volunteer his or her time.

## 3. Provide a written test.

You can do this by simply having people answer written questions, such as: What is a pre amp? Describe EQ? and so on.

## 4. Provide a lab test.

Using software such as Garageband, Cakewalk, Pro Tools, etc., you can provide someone with a multitrack recording and see how they choose to mix it. You can tell a lot about someone's level of experience and taste from this exercise.

**Hot Tip!**

**Consider your sound person a part of the team, a part of the band. He or she is as important as any other link. Also, be sure that you and your team treat your sound person honorably and with respect. Don't demand something; ask for it politely.**

### 5. Provide a live test.

Using your church sound system, create a crisis situation, such as feedback, and have your sound person identify and solve the problem. This test should be executed with you and your sound team only. Don't have the band and a host of people watching. Having said this, sometimes you can have the whole band try to solve feedback issues. This can be fun, plus they'll gain experience and a whole new appreciation for what your sound team is up against.

### 6. Determine the level of experience.

Find out if your sound team members have any prior experience and through your testing determine and rate their levels of experience. This can be your own rating for your own purposes; just find a way to be clear on who knows what.

### 7. Provide training for your sound team.

Looking at a soundboard for the first time, or even the hundredth time, can be daunting. Dealing with feedback issues and all the worship team members' needs during sound check is not an area you can coast on. You're the team's leader, therefore it's your job to seek out ways to provide the best possible training.

### 8. Invest in your gear.

You can have the best voices, guitar, drums, bass, and keys money can buy, but ultimately, you'll only be as good as what people hear. This goes for your audience *and* how well the band can hear each other. Invest in quality sound gear. It will pay big dividends.

### 9. Bring in the big guns!

Don't hesitate to bring in a trusted professional with great references to help you set up your sound system, provide sound reinforcement, and EQ or tune your room. Have your sound team present. Ask questions and make the most of the opportunity for you and your team to learn about your room and your sound system.

**Smart Chapter #12**
# Your Sound Team:
## A Solid Plan + Patience = Success
*Discussion Questions*

1. Assess the quality and maintenance of your current sound system by: poor, fair, good, great.

2. Have you ever provided any kind of questionnaire or test to determine the skill level of your current sound team?

3. Can you confidently comment on the skill level of your current sound team?

4. How is your monitor system? Does it allow everyone to clearly hear each other?

5. How are your mains? Is the audience able to clearly hear the worship band and/or pastor/speakers?

**Hot Tip!**

**Even subtle sound issues can drain and distract the congregation, as well as a speaker, worship leader, and worship team.**

6. Do you have a soundboard and power amp that is sufficient for your needs?

7. Do you have adequate power supply for your sound system?

8. Are you aware of the wiring and power (supply) in your building?

9. How often do you experience crackles, buzzes, and hums?

Remember, even subtle sound issues can drain and distract the congregation, as well as a speaker or worship team. Make a list of your needs and your current budget. Prioritize your list and make a plan to solve the problems.

# Smart Chapter #13
# You're Invited to Play at a Church or Worship Event . . . What Now?

## 1. What is the date, time, and place?

This is the first of all the obvious, but often overlooked, questions you'll need to ask.

## 2. What is the purpose of the gig and what kind of service are they planning (contemporary, traditional, or blended)?

You want to be prepared *and* you want to know if and how you can serve the Lord, the people, and the situation best.

## 3. How long do they want you to play?

This can help you decide if you're the leader for the job and what you need in terms of band and equipment. (Do you really want to drive five hours to play for twenty minutes, even if you are being compensated?)

## 4. Do they know the songs you typically sing or will you need to be prepared with other material?

It's great to ask the worship leader and/or pastor who issued the invitation what songs their congregation has been doing and with which songs they are or are not familiar.

## 5. What is the "personality" of the church as worshipers? Are they exuberant, guarded, etc.?

This will help you begin to pray toward creating the appropriate set list and how God wants you to deliver whatever message in worship He has for you and your team to give away.

**Hot Tip!**

**Write down a list of questions and call the person who invited you. Don't email the questions. You can't convey tone in email, and you want that person to know you are excited about the opportunity to serve, and that is at the heart of each question.**

### 6. Are you expected to speak during the service or at another time while there?

This is *very* helpful to know up front!

### 7. Is this a paid gig or pro bono?

Don't feel you have to apologize for needing an answer to this question. It's a really good thing to ask up front and then just be quiet. It could be as simple as asking, "Is there a budget for this?" Sometimes you just want to bless another worship leader or church and you don't want or need anything. Other times, it's more appropriate to receive compensation for your time and effort. Regardless, it needs to be talked about so everyone and everything is clear. A worker is worth his wage (see Luke 10:7). Even if the gig is pro bono, you still need to know if the church inviting you will cover your expenses.

### 8. Are you using your own players or will you need players from the church or venue where you've been invited to play?

The answer to this question will also help you determine the answer to question number 9. You'll also want to make sure the players you use are qualified to cover the musical territory you plan to cover. There is always give and take with this. Ask the person who is inviting you what level of musicianship his players have and what they are capable of.

### 9. Are you bringing your own sound person or do they have someone who will work for you? Are you bringing your person to run the projector, or do they already have someone?

Same principle as applies to number 8.

### 10. Are you flying or driving?

This can be a determining factor in who and what you can bring with you.

### 11. Who pays the extra baggage for your guitars, pedal board, etc.?

This will most likely involve paperwork that you would hand over along with any other receipts you pass along for reimbursement. Keep good records and save all receipts. It's not cool to say you spent money for something like an extra bag, but then you do not have a receipt for their accountant.

### 12. Where are you staying? If you are bringing a band, where will they stay?

These are great questions to ask early on, especially if you are unfamiliar with the church or venue. They might have budgeted for a hotel or they might have you all spread out in homes. If you need to keep close ties to the band for preparation purposes and you are spread out all over the city, you need to know this ahead of time. Don't expect others to anticipate your needs. You don't have to be high maintenance, but you do need to know these details. You can work within any limitation, but you must be prepared to do it well and with a positive attitude.

### 13. When do you load in? When do you sound check? Have this all worked out before you rehearse your band.

You want an answer to this one because you may have more or less time than you assumed (actually, do *not* assume anything; instead, ask). If you know this ahead of time, it can help you better prepare for what you have to accomplish before getting there.

**Hot Tip!**

**It's almost impossible to over-communicate.**

## Smart Chapter #13
# You're Invited to Play at a Church or Worship Event . . . What Now?
### *Discussion Questions*

1. What is the date, time, and place?

2. What is the purpose of the gig and what kind of service are they planning?

3. How long do they want you to play?

4. Do they know the songs you typically sing or will you need to be prepared with other material?

5. What is the "personality" of the church as worshipers? Are they exuberant, guarded, etc.?

6. Are you expected to speak during the service or at another time while there?

7. Is this a paid gig or pro bono?

8. Are you using your own players or will you need players from the church or venue where you've been invited to play?

9. Are you bringing your own sound person or do they have someone who will work for you?

10. Are you bringing your person to run the projector, or do they already have someone?  What software will the church/venue be using?

11. Are you flying or driving?

12. Who pays the extra baggage for your guitars, pedal board, etc.?

13. Where are you staying? If you are bringing a band, where will they stay?

14. When do you load in? When do you sound check? Have this all worked out before you rehearse your band.

Helpful tip:  Make sure you are A/V compatible, bring all kinds of adaptors.  Don't depend on the church or venue to have the answers to your problems.  Also, plan ahead for a computer crash, bring a backup, (i.e. flash drive, hard copies, etc.).

**Smart Chapter #14**
# You're Inviting a Guest Worship Leader to Your Church

## 1. What is the vision and purpose of the invitation? What is the format for the entire worship service?

Simply put, what is your "why" for the meeting and invitation?

## 2. What is your budget? Can you accomplish your "vision" with the available budget?

If so, then you are ready to move forward with an invitation. Be clear about your purpose, your mission, and how you will be able to compensate your guest.

## 3. When is your guest arriving?

Make sure you communicate the date, time, and place.

## 4. Discuss load in, rehearsal, sound check, and load out.

Cover the "when" for each, how much time is needed, and how many people you'll have helping. Always have more help than you need. Plan for emergencies.

## 5. How many guests will you have—one person or a band?

If you have players who can truly support your guest, this might be a way to help offset the cost. However, make sure you base this decision on your vision and budget. *Sometimes the money you might spend to get a particular person who plays a supportive role to your invited guest (i.e. a guitar player, keyboardist, drummer, etc.), might make all the difference in reaching your goal or no*

**Hot Tip!**

**This seems obvious, but ask questions and over-communicate. Develop a a vision, purpose, or mission statement in the beginning and run all your decisions through it for congruency.**

### 6. What gear does your guest need (i.e., what is the person or band bringing and what are you providing)?

If flying is involved, you might be better off checking into renting some gear, such as guitar amps, etc.

### 7. Where will your guest(s) stay? Are you providing a hotel or someone's home?

Discuss this up front as well, and make sure your guest doesn't have any special needs. Sometimes a person's home can be just the right thing, and sometimes not.

### 8. Will you need to have food prepared, cash or vouchers, or will you or someone you've designated take the guest to eat upon arrival? Will you have a per diem?

Have all these budgetary concerns worked out beforehand so you don't end up searching for cash or a way to feed someone on the spot. *If you are preparing food, make sure you've covered allergies with your guest ahead of time. Also, do they need to keep their receipts?*

### 9. Who will provide the sound person and who will run the projector?

Make sure you are connecting the dots. If your sound person isn't a people person, do what you have to do to make sure the ground is covered, any questions answered, and any potential surprises eliminated.

### 10. Are there any potential requests from your pastor?

Ask the pastor, or whoever is leading the worship event, ahead of time about any expectations (i.e., certain songs, style of worship, theme, etc.). Try to remove any last-minute requests so your guest is adequately prepared.

## 11. Finally, do you have any other expectations or meetings the guest may need to attend?

If so, tell them beforehand so they don't feel worked over.

# Smart Chapter #14
# You're Inviting a Guest Worship Leader to Your Church

*Discussion Questions*

1. What is the vision and purpose of the invitation? What is the format for the entire worship service?

2. What is your budget? Can you accomplish your "vision" with the available budget?

3. When is your guest arriving?

4. Discuss load in, rehearsal, sound check, and load out.

5. How many guests will you have—one person or a band?

6. What gear does your guest need (i.e., what is the person or band bringing and what are you providing)?

7. Where will your guest(s) stay? Are you providing a hotel or someone's home?  Make sure to let them know!!

8. What is the food plan: prepared food on site, cash/vouchers, will you have a designated person taking your guest out to eat?

9. Will you have a per diem?

10. Who will provide the sound person and who will run the projector?

11. Are there any potential requests from your pastor?

12. Finally, do you have any other expectations or meetings the guest may need to attend?

# Musicianship

Play the music, not the instrument.

—Anonymous

## Smart Chapter #15
# Planning Kills Spontaneity . . . Well, Not Exactly!
### *Will Planning for Worship Kill the Flow of the Spirit?*

God can use anybody at anytime. But historically, God has done more, more often, with those who are faithful and prepared.

## 1. True: God loves to inhabit the praises of His people.

Thank God that this is our story and that He loves to be a part of our worship, whether it is messy or not!

## 2. False: God can inhabit our praises more effectively if we don't plan on praising Him.

It sounds silly when you put it that way, doesn't it? But how often are we guilty of this kind of thinking? Take a good look at some of your beliefs and see if you've inadvertently bought into this lie.

## 3. True: The better you know your instrument, the better you can improvise.

Yes, of course. The better you know your instrument, theory, scales, sight reading, etc., the freer you are to express yourself. Knowledge, practice, and precision are your launching pads. Flying by the seat of your pants takes up valuable brain space, individually and collectively, that could be used to listen to the Spirit. Plan your solo or band moments of spontaneity. This allows each person to be prepared to go with the flow when it is time.

## 4. False: The greater your understanding of music theory, the more likely you are to get too heady and forget about God (and "quench" the Spirit).

Sometimes in an effort to not be "religious," we run from discipline. Don't be reactionary; pursue God with your body, soul, mind, and spirit! You would never use this logic with a Christian doctor or teacher or businessman. You *want* them to know their stuff!

### 5. True: If you fail to plan, you plan to fail.

A few people out there believe it's better to just show up and see what happens instead of practicing and rehearsing. Nothing could be further from the truth. It may work for you sometimes, but every set can be better with practice.

### 6. True: The army with the best training, tools, and plans usually wins.

Even in stories where God won battles for the Israelites in supernatural ways, the soldiers brought with them to the field their years of training.

### 7. True: You and your band/worship team are in a war!

A war never goes exactly as planned, but it is *planned for*! Come prepared for the unexpected.

### Hot Tip Extra!

The better you know a song and arrangement, the easier it is for you and your band to break from what you know and then come back into the song after exploring uncharted territory. I once heard a story of two famous actors. Actor A was an accomplished improviser. Actor B (looking forward to a more improvisational approach) decided to do very little in the area of memorization and preparation. However, Actor B soon learned that the secret of Actor A's success at improvisation was his diligence to learn the script backward and forward, so he could leave it anytime, but jump back in and feed the other actors their expected line. This is a great way to approach your preparation with your music, band, vocalists, and worship team.

**Hot Tip!**

**The better you know a song and arrangement, the easier it is for you and your band to break from what you know and then come back into the song after exploring uncharted territory.**

## Smart Chapter #15
# Planning Kills Spontaneity . . .
# Well, Not Exactly!
### *Discussion Questions*

1. True or false?  The one most prepared, educated, and equipped is most often the most capable of being spontaneous during a set.

2. True or false?  The better you know your instrument, the better you can improvise.

3. True or false?  The musician with the most training and practice is the most likely to succeed.  If this is true, what is your plan to ensure that you are going to succeed at being the very best you can be with what God has given you?

# Smart Chapter #16
# Memorization

Memorization takes time and there is no easy way around it. Having the lyrics and the music memorized will help your worship team focus on what's important.

## 1. Know your lyrics.

Work toward committing songs to memory, but don't underestimate the value of a projector, video screen, teleprompters, and music stands dedicated to the stage. Still, preparation is a must so no one goes blank during the performance.

## 2. Make sure everyone has an MP3 of the song.

Being able to hear and "live with the song" the week before is a sure way to help everyone commit the song to memory.

## 3. Know the melody—no reason to miss on this.

By the time of the event, you should have gone through all the songs numerous times at home and rehearsals.

## 4. Know your vocal harmony parts.

The better you are prepared, the better you sound. Hard work and dedication always pay off. Committing to this will prevent vocals from dropping out or stumbling around for parts. Work out harmonies and vocal parts without a sound system and without the band. This will help you blend and avoid needless holdups in practice.

## 5. Play the song acoustically.

Let's say, for instance, you are an electric guitar player. If so, try picking up an acoustic guitar and playing through the song at home

**Hot Tip!**

**Anything you can do to give your team an advantage—charts, sheet music, tele-prompters, projectors, or video screens—should not be discounted. The more comfortable your team is, the more they can lose themselves in worship!**

without the band or track. This exercise will further assist you in "getting your head" around the tune.

### 6. Chord charts—a must!

Always be ready with chord charts for all band/team members. If everyone can flip to a chart for a last-minute change, you're covered. It is also a good idea to create song chart books. Then specific players in your worship team/band rotation will have their notations already written down from one gig to the next.

### 7. Rehearse without the chart.

If it seems needful, take time in your rehearsal and have everyone play without charts. Getting everyone's head out of the books will help everyone focus more on what they are hearing.

### 8. Prepare for complicated turns and riffs.

Some musicians who don't have a strong ear will require a more detailed chord chart or number chart to accurately perform a certain lick, musical phrase, or tricky turn. Use the tools that make every team member feel at ease, confident, and comfortably prepared.

## Smart Chapter #16
# Memorization
*Discussion Questions*

1. What is a good idea to give to your players before the gig to help everyone commit the song to memory?



2. What is a helpful tip to help the band/team focus more on hearing?



3. The goal is to use any and every tool you can to make your band/team feel_____ , _____ , and _____ prepared.

## Smart Chapter #17
# Preparation

I will study and prepare and perhaps my chance will come.
—Abraham Lincoln

## 1. Practice what you play.

Your performance should be a reflection of your rehearsals. Poor rehearsals that include bad habits, such as tardiness, lack of effort, and an overall "wing it" mentality, are sure to creep their way into the performance. Practice does make perfect!

## 2. Pray before you play.

Rehearsals and performances should always begin with prayer. Make rehearsals another opportunity to connect with Jesus. Get the focus off you and your team and put it where it belongs—on Jesus!

## 3. Select the proper songs—that's 50 percent of your success.

Selected songs must always meet the criteria your event dictates. "Wrong choice of song" is a common term heard on *American Idol* and usually with good reason. Sometimes it's 100 percent of the reason for a poor performance and lack of connection with the audience or congregation. Make sure your songs fit the event, your voice, the audience, and the message that will be presented overall.

## 4. Add originality.

Try to make the song sound fresh by changing some basic things, like intros, beat, and phrasing. Be sure to have someone who is honest and skilled in music give you advice on your interpretation of the song. This is important because we all have ideas in our head that don't work when we try to flesh them out. The deeper you bury your identity in Christ, the more courage you'll have to express your originality . . . and take criticism when needed. Be brave and go for something fresh . . . but be humble and keep your roots grounded in Jesus!

## 5. Don't try to fix what is not broken.

Once the team has perfected a song, avoid spending unnecessary time on it and move on to the next selection. Overworking a song will lead to fatigue and cause the team to lose interest. You must help to facilitate a smooth rehearsal, one that keeps the team's interest high. Maintain energy and expectation with your team and your tune choices.

## 6. Practice, practice, practice!

You should take time out daily to work on your craft. This is part of the preparation process and each member of the team will benefit from it. You are only as good as your weakest link.

## 7. Allow the songs to become second nature.

Ultimately, the songs should be delivered without having to think about them. You will know when you have hit this point in preparation. When you have, everything comes with ease and flows seamlessly. *Remember, this is the goal you are shooting for; it's impractical to think this will always be the case.*

## 8. Make sure your gear is ready to go.

Avoid needless holdups due to shorted-out cords, blown tubes, etc. Test your guitars, amps, pedal boards, and cords earlier in the day before practice, so you have enough time to take care of whatever needs attention and you're ready to roll for rehearsal and/or your gig.

**Hot Tip!**

**As the team's chemistry evolves, there will come a time when picking up a new song may come quickly and easily. Moments like these don't get much better, but they are few and far between. Do not assume other songs will come that easily for future events.**

## Smart Chapter #17
# Preparation
*Discussion Questions*

1. Your performance should reflect your what?

2. When is a great time to pray with your band/team?

3. You can keep an old song fresh by doing what?

4. How can you help to avoid needless holdups?

5. Song _____ can be crucial to your success.

6. Overworking a song can lead to what?

## Smart Chapter #18
# The Guitar Player's Checklist

### 1. Nine-volt batteries . . . check.

All it takes is a few gigs to know you have to be packing 9-volt batteries. If everything falls apart, you can at least power your tuner and compressor.

### 2. Extra sets of strings . . . check.

Make sure you are covered in case you break a string, but have an extra set or two in case someone else on the team breaks one too.

### 3. Picks . . . check.

Picks disappear like socks in the dryer. Any little mint or lozenge tin, like Sucrets or Altoids, makes a great case for your picks. Also, keep picks with different thicknesses/gauge in case someone asks for a different type sound from you. A different gauge can assist you in getting a brighter or duller and darker sound.

### 4. Capo . . . check.

If you've played worship music for any length of time, you are familiar with the capo. (See smart chapter # 19 on capo do's and don'ts.)

### 5. Guitar strap . . . check.

Try locking straps on your guitar. It's a great way to keep your strap from sliding off while you are playing and will usually ensure that you don't leave your strap at home.

### 6. Extra cables . . . check.

Always have extra cables on hand for your pedals, your guitar, and for someone else who's having an emergency.

**Hot Tip!**

**Did you forget your strap? Check this out . . . take a roll of duct tape and stretch two pieces out about six inches longer than the length of a guitar strap and stick them together (sticky sides in). Double the ends over about an inch and a half to strengthen the eyelets, poke a hole through on each end, and you're ready to roll.**

### 7. Peg winder . . . check.

A peg winder is a great way to help you change strings fast.

### 8. Snips, small screwdrivers, and wire pliers . . . check.

Make sure you have tools handy for any little job you need for your guitar, pedals, etc.

### 9. Small tackle box or satchel . . . check.

Purchase some type of box or container where you can neatly store your batteries, strings, picks, cables, peg winder, screwdrivers, etc.

### 10. Power up your pedal board . . . check.

Power up your pedal board and make sure you are getting signal through it. Double-check all your cables for wear and tear.

### 11. Power up your amp . . . check.

Take a cable and go straight to your amp to make sure you are getting a signal.

### 12. Extra guitars . . . check.

Now, you might be in a place where all you can afford is one guitar and that's fine. However, when you have two or more guitars, be sure to have that second guitar ready to go in case you break a string during your performance and need an alternative right away.

### 13. Guitar stand . . . check.

It's always better not to rely on someone else to provide your guitar stand or stands. Cover yourself. If one is provided, you can leave yours in the car.

## 14. Music stand . . . check.

Same point for #13 applies to your music stand. If you need one, be prepared with your own. Also, you might want to check out a small, battery-powered, clip-on light for your music stand, like the K&M Twin-Headed Music Stand Light, the Mighty Bright XtraFlex Duet LED Music Light, or something similar. They are small, convenient, and easy to use.

**Smart Chapter #18**
# The Guitar Player's Checklist

☐   Nine volt batteries

☐   Extra strings

☐   Picks

☐   Capo

☐   Guitar strap

☐   Extra cables

☐   Peg winder

☐   Snips, small screwdriver, wire pliers, etc

☐   Power up your pedal board

☐   Power up your amp

☐   Extra guitar

☐   Guitar stand or stands

☐   Music stand

☐   Clip-on light for your music stand

# Smart Chapter #19
# The Do's and Don'ts of the Capo

Like most of you, I thank God for the capo. The bottom line with music is you want to enjoy playing it, and when getting started, the capo lets you jump in and do just that. Here are a few do's and don'ts (regarding the capo) as you progress in your playing.

## 1. Do use the capo to explore the neck.

Check this out. If you are playing a song in a particular key and your capo is on the second fret, look at what your fingers are doing and where they are placed. Now think of your first finger on your fret hand as the capo, remove the capo and try to play that same chord. You can try this regardless of what fret your capo is on. Now try losing the capo all together and play the song without it.

## 2. Don't let the capo turn into a dependant crutch.

Force yourself to learn to play in multiple keys. Don't use the capo in such a way that you are always using the same fingering for chord formations.

## 3. Do use the capo to broaden the sonic spectrum.

If another guitar is playing open chords at the end of the neck, it might be a good opportunity to use the capo higher on the neck, so you can play in a higher register away from the lower open chord spectrum.

## 4. Don't use the capo in the same place every time.

Play the same song with your capo is several different places. This will force you to think outside the box and learn the neck in the process.

**Hot Tip!**

For fun, you might want to try some of the partial capos out there. Sometimes people use a standard capo in conjunction with a partial capo to create an open tuning or a different sound and color.

### 5. Do use the capo for color.

The capo played up high on the neck can produce a certain attitude, buoyancy, and expectancy. The song "Here Comes the Sun" (with capo on the seventh fret) is a perfect example of how a capo can create a mood.

## Smart Chapter #19
# The Do's and Don'ts of the Capo
### *Discussion Questions*

1. How often do you use a capo?

2. Are you able to play a song in a different key without using a capo?

3. What are some things you can use the capo for?

4. When using the capo, what should you avoid?

# Smart Chapter #20
# Phrasing
*The making of a musical statement*

When performing, you want every note to count. Phrasing is all about *how you deliver* each note. Take the time to think your song through. Here are a few tips.

## 1. Make each note count.

Play each part with the same effort and level of concentration (don't check out). Complicated bunches of notes put together to show off your knowledge of the mechanics doesn't make you musical. Remember, as a player, the ultimate goal is to make the song shine.

## 2. What you don't play is often as important as what you do play.

Play, and even more importantly, give space where needed.

## 3. Develop style in your playing.

If you are a guitar player, give your instrument a voice by listening to great singers or horn players. Memorable solos sound like the instrument is a singer. There is space to breathe, move, and articulate a phrase by developing your style and incorporating it into your songs.

## 4. Use the appropriate scales.

Using an inappropriate scale or mode will disrupt the meaning and vibe of the song. Applying a scale that fits the particular style of song you're playing will help you develop more effective phrasing.

## 5. Record yourself.

This is where you will truly find out how effective your phrasing, style, note choice, and taste really are. After you hear what you've done, you will more readily recognize the improvements you need to make.

### 6. Increase your musical vocabulary.

Listening to quality music performed by great artists will create a solid library of music in your head. This will transfer to your own style as you continue to grow in your gift. Phrasing will become noticeably better when you surround yourself with great music.

### 7. Utilize double stops/chord fragments.

Experimenting with double stops/chord fragments (two to three notes of a chord) is a powerful way to accentuate and enhance your phrasing.

**Hot Tip!**

**The more musicians you have playing in the band, the more important it will be for each player to listen more and play less.**

## Smart Chapter #20
# Phrasing
### *Discussion Questions*

1. Phrasing is all about _____ you deliver each note.


2. Even as a guitar player, there is space to _____ , _____ , and _____ a phrase.


3. Have you ever recorded yourself playing or singing so you can listen back objectively?


4. Give a description of ways you create space in your playing.


5. In your next rehearsal, take time to focus your energy on listening. Describe the outcome.


6. Do you feel nervous or uncomfortable leaving space?  Why?

## Smart chapter #21
# Intonation
*Ability to sing/play in tune.*

*Intonation* is the pitch and tone of your voice or instrument. A variety of factors can affect proper pitch and tone. Practice the following techniques for excellent intonation.

## 1. Pay attention.

This is really a big part of the battle. So many things compete for your attention (playing in time, playing the right notes, monitor mix, excitement, fear, etc,), so learn to give attention to your tone. As a singer your tone is all you. As a player a big part of your tone is actually found in your fingers.

## 2. Practice singing on pitch.

This is important! Record yourself singing alone, with and without an instrument. After judging the recording, be mindful of the areas in which you need to improve your pitch and try again. Be persistent, and through hard work you should be able to fix your intonation.

## 3. Take lessons.

A good vocal/musician coach can offer great benefits to fixing any intonation challenges you're facing. Quality pros are trained in these areas and can really assist you. Roger Federer was the number-one ranked tennis player in the world for years and has won more majors than anyone else in history—and he still has a coach. Imagine that! It is always a positive thing to continue with lessons.

## 4. Purchase a quality instrument and have it set up by a professional.

Great musicians use quality gear. The right gear and tone can make the difference between sounding as if you play with authority or

**Hot Tip!**

**When you are in rehearsals or a certain venue, nothing is more distracting than that one person who is flat or out of tune. . . . Set the tone by keeping your intonation spot on!**

sounding wimpy. Like anything important and valuable, your instrument will need regular maintenance and attention by a professional.

### 5. Exercise your God-given gift.

Your voice, fingers, and feet are all used to create music and should be exercised daily. If you ran one mile only one day per week, would you ever be in shape? No, you'd struggle each time you ran. Your musical gift needs to be worked daily too. Your ear will then become familiar with good sound and pitch, and you'll improve your overall intonation.

### 6. Warm up and tune up regularly.

Take the proper time to warm up. Your instrument should be tuned up and ready to go right before rehearsals, services, and any other music venues you are participating in. As with any muscle, cold, heat, sudden changes in temperature, travel, etc.—all affect performance and pitch. Pay attention, prepare, and adjust accordingly.

## Smart chapter #21
# Intonation
### *Discussion Questions*

1. Do you have trouble singing or playing in pitch?

2. Have you ever taken lessons on your instrument of choice? Voice, guitar, etc.?

3. If you are a guitar or bass player, how often do you have your instrument serviced and set up?

4. Do you regularly warm up before practicing or performing?

# Smart Chapter #22
# Vocal Clarity

Articulation, enunciation of words, projecting with the correct inflection and control are all an important part of an effective worship set.

## 1. Energy is everything—sing with enthusiasm and passion.

Do not take any song for granted. My vocal coach once told me, "Sing every song as if it's the first time anyone has ever heard it."

## 2. Avoid lazy phrasing.

The audience will be taking their cues from you. Try to give every section of a song the same care. Great talent and ability still require great effort. Some professional athletes have the negative reputation of taking numerous plays off during a game. A singer must not take certain phrases off in a song either. Your pitch can turn flat in an instant, so avoid being lazy.

## 3. Pronunciation of words—keep the message of the song clear.

A worship leader is a little bit like a choir director, and people will be queuing off of your pronunciation, phrasing, and delivery. The message must be clear and the phrasing must be able to be followed. Make sure your words and phrasing can be understood and duplicated.

## 4. Sing with the song, not against it!

A song with a full band, and perhaps an orchestra, requires you to sing to a higher level of energy and volume. Doing the same song with just an acoustic guitar requires you to adjust your phrasing, volume, and tone. Passion remains the same, but you have to keep the song in balance with the style in which you are singing it, the type of instruments used, and the feeling you seek to evoke with that particular worship song.

## 5. Avoid oversinging.

Too much ad-libbing, overpronunciation of lyrics, and sustaining notes can give your audience ear fatigue. You don't want to be like a guitar player who thinks he is the only one playing in the song. Eventually, everyone wants to turn him off. The same goes for vocalists. Always serve the song.

**Hot Tip!**

**Recording your songs will allow you to hear back what you would change if you did the song again. This is a great way to train your ear and your technique to better become a seasoned vocalist.**

## Smart Chapter #22
# Vocal Clarity
### *Discussion Questions*

1. "Sing every song as if it's the _____ _____ anyone has ever heard it."

2. Do you stay focused and present while singing, or do you allow your mind to drift?

3. Do you practice consistency in how you lead songs, or do you have the habit of changing up the melodies?

4. Do you have lazy or articulate phrasing?

5. Do you prompt the congregation with the words that are coming next?

**Hot Tip!**

**Be careful. Sometimes a little change can keep something fresh, but you can also lose your audience by doing this!**

## Smart Chapter #23
# Breathing

Nothing will help your vocal performance like learning to breathe properly. Correct breathing will affect the tone quality, sustainability, and pitch of vocals, as well as the tone of woodwind and brass players, making your songs more effective in reaching the audience as you lead in worship. Breath control is not only for vocalists and woodwind/brass musicians; it will also help instrumentalists relax and play more effectively. Here are some suggestions for learning to breathe properly before you ever hit the stage to lead in worship.

## 1. Stay loose.

Vocalists and musicians who breathe properly are much more relaxed. Take note as you are playing. When you get a solo, do you hold your breath or are you relaxed and breathing normally?

## 2. Guitar, bass, keys and drums.

Even though you don't have to take a breathing break, the listener needs one from time to time. Think of your instrument as a horn and take "breaths" in your phrasing.

## 3. Take deep breaths.

Do this during your prayer time to maintain focus. Onstage your breathing should be relaxed and steady.

## 4. Vocal coaching.

Singers should seek a vocal coach and take lessons to further shape their voices. It is amazing what a difference some professional coaching and practice can make with any voice. You can study for years, or if you are on a tight budget, just take a few lessons. Either way, coaching can make a tremendous difference and increase the quality of your singing voice and performance.

**Hot Tip!**

**Focusing on the act of breathing clears the mind of all daily distractions, enabling us to better connect with the Spirit within.**

**—Author Unknown**

### 5. Words to live by.

"Fear less, hope more; eat less, chew more; whine less, *breathe more*; talk less, say more; hate less, love more" (Swedish proverb, emphasis mine).

### Onstage and off.

Thinking about your breathing outside of musical situations is important too. Practice deep breathing in the morning when you wake up, at night when you go to bed, during a workout, or when you are in any given stressful situation—all will help you relax and make you more effective in your music as well.

## Smart Chapter #23
# Breathing
*Discussion Questions*

1. Do you have a tendency to get tight, or do you stay loose when leading and singing?

2. Do you find yourself breathing regularly or holding your breath for excessive amounts of time?

3. Are you winded at the end of a service or performance?

4. Do you rush onto stage, or do you take a minute or two to dial down, focus in, and breath before going onstage?

# Worship Team and Band

We all need somebody to lean on.
—Bill Withers

## Smart Chapter #24
# Keep the Band Tight
# and the Relationships Right

### 1. Forgive, forgive, forgive.

Nothing robs you of energy faster than resentment. The worst thing about keeping someone locked up in your own personal dungeon of unforgiveness is that you're the only dungeon guard you've got. What a waste of time! In reality, you're the only one missing out on the sunlight because you can't really hold anybody down. Jesus said to "forgive your enemies and pray for those who persecute you." How much more should we practice forgiveness with our worship team/ bandmates. Being in the worship team/band together is sacred. It's family.

### 2. Play, pray, play, pray.

The band that *plays* and *prays* together . . . *goes places*! Yeah okay, you get to stay together too, but you get to *go places*. (That's what makes the music so fun, right?) Make time for rehearsals and make time for prayer. Don't forget your players are coming in with needs too. Taking a moment to find out what the needs are, praying for each other, and then praying for the rehearsal time and worship service are crucial to long-term success!

### 3. Laugh, laugh, laugh.

This is crucial. Laugh during rehearsal, laugh after rehearsal, laugh at yourself when you make a silly mistake. Don't forget your joy. The joy of the Lord is *your strength*! Besides, taking the whole thing too seriously takes years off your life, and you've got too much living to do!

### 4. Eat, eat, eat.

A special closeness happens when you break bread together. So enjoy and celebrate each other. Eating together is also a great opportunity to spend time with the team's extended family, i.e., spouses, sound people, PowerPoint person, etc.

## 5. Communicate—face to face, phone calls, text, email, Facebook!

The point is, *stay connected.* As a worship leader, you need to facilitate this. Follow each other on Twitter; start a Facebook group; make phone calls to ask, "How are you doing today?" Don't let rehearsal time and Sunday be your only connection points.

## 6. Help each other shine.

Think "team"! For a worship team, the sum is always greater than the parts.

## 7. Exercise healthy boundaries.

Every relationship can cross a line or two; that's what growing is all about. Don't be afraid to respectfully and lovingly define or redefine the boundaries of your relationships as needed.

## 8. Don't just get there together, go there together (think "carpool").

The things you do together, in between playing together, find their way into the music. It all adds up, so enjoy the journey and the destination!

## 9. Know thy bandmate.

David and his "mighty men" lived life together. Living in caves together while running from King Saul can create a bond . . . *fast*! While that may not be your story, you and your band *are* going into battle together. You will find that you fight better together when you know who is covering your back.

**Hot Tip!**

**Taking the time to get to know each other will go a long way toward what you sound like on Sunday, or any day, for that matter.**

## Smart Chapter #24
# Keep the Band Tight
# and the Relationships Right
### *Discussion Questions*

1. Do you practice the act of forgiving regularly?

2. Is there someone right now that you know you need to forgive?

3. Getting together to practice is important, but taking real time to pray for each others' needs can be just as important. Can you write down the last time your band/worship team prayed together?

4. Are you currently aware of personal needs that you can pray for?

5. It's important to stay connected! List some ways you are currently communicating and staying connected with your band/team.

6. Do you only text and email, or do you also spend time phoning and meeting with your band/team?

## Smart Chapter #25
# God Is in the Details
*(We're Talking about Your Rehearsal)*

## 1. Knowledge is empowering, and information will help your team relax and look forward to what is ahead.

You'd be surprised at how a team/band member's mood can "go downhill" en route to a rehearsal if they are confused, anxious, frustrated, and/or unclear about the details.

## 2. Communicate where, when, and for how long the rehearsals will be scheduled.

It's best to be definitive on all three of these so people can schedule their world around it. Have some flexibility, but do your best to keep to the schedule. Start times and stop times can be very important for people with families and busy schedules.

## 3. Talk with your pastor to make sure you are on the same page with his mission and message for the coming Sunday.

You need continuity! Stay in contact with your pastor. Get on the same page with him about the upcoming message. Find songs in your repertoire that support the sermon/teaching. Think of yourself as an extension of what he is trying to accomplish. (*Note*: Engage in your relationship with him. Share your thoughts and ideas. Support him with your encouragement and prayers.)

## 4. Pray over the meeting and song choice for Sunday.

Sounds simple, but how often do we forget to do it? Ask God to guide you as you make the song choices for Sunday. As you ponder what you and your pastor have talked about, take time to listen to God.

**Hot Tip!**

**Take a lesson from one who is arguably the greatest American president who ever lived. Stay in contact with your team and win the rehearsal war!**

### 5. Designate a person to contact the team (email, phone call, reminders).

Keep your communication with the team functional yet personable. It's good to have a system of scheduled times and emails, but it doesn't hurt to have someone double-checking with team members to avoid any unexpected surprises that might arise.

### 6. Who needs to be there and what should they bring?

Communicate who's rehearsing and when. A good idea to save time is to have the singers show up an hour early and work out the parts with them in a smaller room (without sound system and/or distractions). This way you don't have to work out sound issues and can dial in the parts. Then have the band show up the next hour and everyone can work together. Make sure everyone knows what he or she needs to bring.

### 7. Prepare charts and MP3s beforehand.

Email charts and mp3s beforehand to the singers and players so they can learn and live with the songs.

### 8. Communicate what's expected.

So team members have the charts and MP3s, but what exactly is expected of them? How do they prepare? Should they play it exactly as written or played on the MP3? Do they have some creative license? *Warning*: Don't put yourself, or your band members, in a situation where the player has learned the part as it is on the MP3, only to find out at the rehearsal that you have a different idea all together. Ouch!

### 9. Abe Lincoln knew a thing or two.

During the Civil War, President Abraham Lincoln spent significant amounts of time circulating among the troops and would often take trips to the War Department's Telegraph Office. The reason being, he knew communication was vitally important to winning the war. Take a lesson from one who is arguably the greatest American president who ever lived. Stay in contact with your team and win the rehearsal war!

## Smart Chapter #25
# God Is in the Details
*Discussion Questions*

1. Honestly, do you over- or undercommunicate with your band/team?

2. As a worship leader, how connected do you stay to your pastor with what messages are coming up?

3. If you are a weekly worship pastor/leader, do you ponder and pray through songs for Sunday or not?

4. As a worship leader, are you a detailed person? If not, do you know a person whose strength is in the details? And can they help you regularly?

5. Does the band/worship team know what's expected of them at rehearsals? At performances?

6. Do you regularly supply charts and MP3s to your band/team?

## Smart Chapter #26
# Eight Ways to Listen
### *(Because Perspective Is Everything!)*

## 1. Use your monitor mix.

We tend to fill our monitor mix with ourselves. This is not a good habit. Make sure you are using the mix to listen to more players than yourself. Probably the most important part of your monitor mix is being able to hear the drummer (the time keeper). Add the rest of the band in from there, making sure you have a strong representation of the rhythm section and the band leader's vocals and instrument.

## 2. Check the front house sound.

Often the best thing you can do during a rehearsal is to step off the stage and walk out to the soundboard. Go to the front of the house and listen to the mains. Remember, what your mix engineer is hearing is what everybody else will be hearing.

## 3. Close your eyes.

It's a simple trick, but whether you are struggling or just "trucking along," take a second and close your eyes. You're guaranteed to hear something you weren't hearing before.

## 4. Look around.

You might be more visual than you are aural. This is true for many people. If that's true for you, it will help to see what someone is doing as well as hear them. Once you see them, the visual imprint can be translated to what you are hearing and give you a bigger picture of the overall effectiveness of the songs you lead in your worship service.

**Hot Tip!**

**Another note on turning down volume. As a band/ worship team, if you can turn down to a low volume and still make what you are doing powerful and emotional, while keep ing a steady and strong rhythm, you'll be that much better for it when you turn up the volume again.**

### 5. Stand by one of your players.

It can do wonders to hear the sound from one of your band member's perspective. Sometimes the difference is so drastic you'll think you're listening to another band. After listening to what he is hearing in his mix or just standing with him, go back to your spot and see how this changes your perspective.

### 6. Power down.

Sit around with an acoustic guitar, acoustic piano, a bass turned way down, and a djembe. This is a great way to work out arrangements. It forces you to think about parts and keeps you from using volume (as a "crutch"), instead of excellence, to pull people into your worship set.

### 7. Have a player play his or her part alone.

Are you having trouble catching a part someone is playing? Have that person (bass, keys, guitar, etc.) play that part alone without the band. Then have him or her play the part with the whole band playing along. See how it changes your perspective. Sometimes a little, hidden part someone is playing might end up being a feature or "signature" part of the song, so take the time to hear what your band members are actually doing.

### 8. Turn the volume way down.

When everyone in the band/worship team turns down to a very low volume, it forces everyone to really listen and play together, and it will give you a better idea of how well you've mastered the song.

## Smart Chapter #26
# Eight Ways to Listen
*Discussion Questions*

1. Which one of the eight ways to listen do you find most helpful and why?

2. Does your band ever sit down and go through a song acoustically?

3. Do you ever try practicing with a very low volume?

4. Do you as a band/team ever record your rehearsals and then take time to sit down and listen to what you're doing?

5. Remember: When evaluating the expression of your team on their instruments, you should stay encouraging and loving. We are all on a journey and everyone needs room to grow. Vulnerability only comes easily in a safe environment.

## Smart Chapter #27
# Energy

*Be committed to your passion—give it your all!*

Giving your best when it comes time to actually lead a worship service or event is not solely dependent upon how prepared you are musically. You must be ready with your full potential of energy as well.

## 1. Wake up and begin the day going through things in your mind.

Have a clear mind-set as you prepare to minister. Prayer is a great way to begin your day and to increase your energy level. As a musician, you can use your instrument to pray. Either singing or playing while you pray will warm up your spirit and your body for the job ahead.

## 2. Stay clear! Don't surround yourself with people and situations that drag you down.

Especially avoid any programming, activities, or people that tend to leave you feeling bad or disconnected from God. If you are married, stay alert to the fact that quarrels are an easy way to get thrown off. Do your best to use self-control and not pick up an offense as you are prepping to lead worship.

## 3. Choose a healthy diet.

Physically, you want to feel your best, so avoid foods that can cause you to suddenly have an energy crash. Also, make sure you have some fruit, an energy bar, or a drink that can pick you up before you play.

## 4. Be thankful.

Focus on God and give Him thanks for the opportunity to serve. Focus on what is going right and don't let the few little things that aren't coming together steal the moment. You've done your job and you're prepared. Now it's time to jump in and enjoy the moment!

**Hot Tip!**

**Stay present. Thinking about anything other than what you are presently doing will rob you of the energy and focus you need at the moment!**

### 5. Arrive early.

This is a great time to warm up and go over anything you feel needs attention. It also helps you dial into the room, connect with the sound and video personnel, and just get settled before things start hopping. Also, the prayer team usually shows up early, so you can share any needs with them before it gets too crazy. All in all, arriving early really enhances your ability to build relationships and enjoy the process.

### 6. Commit to your opening song.

Your commitment will translate to the audience and they will be more likely to follow with confidence.

### 7. Passion radiates energy.

The two go together and are extremely effective to the audience.

### 8. Finish strong.

Finish with the same commitment with which you began. Even if something hasn't gone completely smoothly, stay focused and on track, leading the audience into God's presence.

## Smart Chapter #27
# Energy
### *Discussion Questions*

1. What do you think about when you first wake up?  Are you excited, hopeful, desperate, anxious, hurried?

2. What are some things you can do to ensure that you have time to wake up and face each day with hope?

3. Do your friends encourage and spur you on, or do they discourage you and distract you from your goals?

4. Do you eat healthy?  How many healthy meals do you eat ach week?

5. Remember this: Write down ten things you are thankful for and keep them with you this week.  Pull them out each day to read and thank God for them.

## Smart Chapter #28
# Blend: Creating a Balanced Sound

Say it loud, say it clear, you can listen as well as you hear.
—Mike Rutherford and B. A. Robertson

To create great balance among the team as you lead through your worship songs, follow these suggestions.

## 1. Listening is more important than playing.

Each team member must be aware and listening to what everyone else on the team is doing. What you hear is more important than what you play. What you hear determines what you play. With a band and a worship team, the sum is always greater than is parts, so listen to what is going on around you!

## 2. Be aware of dynamics.

Everyone must pay attention when the band as a whole is increasing or decreasing in volume to ensure you are moving together with order among the musicians and vocalists. Blend on the way up and on the way down.

## 3. Don't overload your sound person.

The better your team blends together, the less work your sound person will have to do. Vocalists, use breath control and the space between your mouth and the microphone to control your volume. Musicians, avoid overattacking your instruments, which causes quick bursts in volume. You should invest in a good compressor/limiter to avoid this as well. As a player and a band, you should be the ones controlling your dynamics, not your sound person.

**Hot Tip!**

**Make a habit to keep watching and listening to each other in rehearsal and onstage. The issue of blending must be mastered during rehearsals. Record your team and listen to yourselves.**

### 4. Conduct a stage sound check.

Doing a proper sound check will help everyone blend. This means you have to have more than just you in your monitor. You must hear each other in order to blend properly.

### 5. Be aware of complicated turns and riffs.

All it takes is a missed turnaround to send your team/band in all different directions. Take time in your rehearsal to execute turnarounds and riffs to facilitate the blend when onstage.

## Smart Chapter #28
# Blend: Creating a Balanced Sound
### *Discussion Questions*

1. Does your band/team have a good blend?

2. Is your band/team able to grow and decrease in volume together smoothly? Are you all able to grow and decrease in intensity together smoothly?

3. Are you or is one of your band/team members always louder than everyone else?

4. A big part of the battle for blend is hearing. What can you do (sound system, monitors, practice, rehearsals) to hear each other better?

5. Practice celebrating each other as musicians. Encourage each other with what you really liked in their playing

## Smart Chapter #29
# Dynamics
*Effective use of contrasting volumes*

Few songs are performed at the same dynamic level throughout. The ebbs and flows of volume in songs convey certain moods and emotions to the audience. Dynamics, executed well in a song, help drive home the feeling and message you want to get across to your audience. They also keep your audience engaged from song to song. Try these tips to keep the dynamics of your songs in a worship event flowing up and down effortlessly and effectively.

## 1. Kick out the crutch (and turn off your sound system).

Logistically speaking, the most powerful moments in music are not derived from volume, but rather unity and groove. Unity and groove are only found through listening. That's right, listening is one of the most powerful tools you have in music. Set up your band/team close together, mic the vocalist, and make everyone else play through small amps or acoustically. This forces everyone to play at a lower volume so they can hear the other people (something we almost all need to be doing anyway). Discipline yourself to play with energy and authority, but at a whisper. It can be done and it will take the delivery of your song to a completely new level.

## 2. Unity and groove are only found through listening.

That's right, listening is one of the most powerful tools you have in music. Yes, this was stated in point 1, but it is worth repeating!

*More on this*: Each team member must be aware of what everyone else on the team is doing. Honestly, a great band experience is like a great "hang"—everyone *must* be heard and enjoyed for who they are in the band and what they bring to the experience. Strive to build members who listen to each other so that the band develops confidence in the abilities of each member. This history of listening

**Hot Tip!**

**With regard to volume, always give yourself some headroom, meaning don't start a song at a 10 on a scale of 1–10 (volume wise). Following this tip will give your song room to grow into the chorus and/or bridge.**

will allow the team to perfect the dynamics in each song. And building trust through listening to each other will really impact your effectiveness onstage. It will also give you greater enjoyment during your live sets. Just think about it—if you know your buddies are really listening to you, you want to play better. A tasty lick from one player inspires every other player to play with sensitivity as well! Also, beautiful, unified playing creates an amazing launching pad for singers to break out with spontaneous Spirit-led ad libs as well, especially when they feel the safety of a sensitive, listening band. All this good chemistry will spill over to excitement and a deep experience for your audience.

### 3. Play in time together.

Encourage the bass player and drummer to spend time practicing together. Also, have the band practice without the vocals and then have the vocals practice without the band. Half the battle of playing together is hearing each other, and the other half is knowing what the other player/singer is going to do (even before you hear it). This comes with time. Putting these simple exercises into practice will help you all play together better in time and will increase your dynamic capability.

### 4. Synchronize volume swells.

Everyone must pay attention when performing volume swells to ensure the increase in volume goes up together with order. The same thing applies when bringing a song down in volume to a quieter moment. The dynamics of volume changes must be done together to properly reinforce the impact and message of the song.

### 5. Help your sound person.

See smart chapter #28, Blend.

### 6. Be aware of dynamics during your stage sound check.

Work on your team's dynamics during the sound check to ensure that everyone can hear each other well. Issues can be resolved when you do so.

## 7. Be aware of turnarounds.

It can be easy when working on a song to overlook the turnaround. Make your turnarounds count whether you are creating space, increasing volume, decreasing volume, etc. Don't take the turnaround off. Stay connected. Also, a little hint, typically people are focusing on what's ahead and not the turnaround itself. This can cause you to rush the tempo. Make sure you are playing the notes at hand and not the notes to come.

## 8. Work toward dynamic vocals.

Staying together whether singing vibrato or straight tone will help your dynamics flow more smoothly. Avoid having half the team singing with vibrato and the other half singing without it.

# Smart Chapter #29
# Dynamics
*Discussion Questions*

1. If your band/team pulls back to a whisper in volume, do you lose power? If so, why? Does your tempo fall apart? If so, why?

2. Does your band/team support the vocalist effectively or do they have a habit of drowning the vocals out? Do your players encourage the vocalists and help them to feel a part of the group?

3. Does your band/team practice volume swells together?

4. Does your band/team speed up or slow down going into a chorus or turn around? If so, why?

## Smart Chapter #30
# Musical Transitions

A large part of what makes for an effective worship experience is how the songs flow from one to the other. Here are some suggestions for keeping your musical transitions smooth.

## 1. Work on transitions during rehearsal.

If you sense that your transitions in rehearsal are sticky, then they are! Work this out as a team and smooth it out.

## 2. Keep transitions short and smooth.

Keep the transitions short, especially during the high-energy material! You want to capture everyone's attention while you have it, and too much delay at the beginning of an event will cause minds to wander.

## 3. Think about the sequence of songs and the keys they are in.

In this modern age where everything gets edited and our minds are bombarded with quickly changing images and sounds, enjoy the freedom you have as a worship leader to create a journey for your audience. Avoid making your transitions choppy, especially when moving into midtempo and slower songs. Test yourself and your team in rehearsal by transitioning the end of one song in your set into the beginning of the next song. Part of your ministry to your congregation is creating a smooth, worshipful place where their souls can rest and meet with the Holy Spirit. Your transitions are important for this to happen.

## 4. Think of your set as a story.

Here's another good approach. Think of your worship set as a fluid journey or all one story with different chapters. Once people enter in, continue to foster and create expectation for what's coming.

**Hot Tip!**

**Don't always try to incorporate every aspect of this chapter in every one of your sets. Certain sets might be characterized by only one or two of the points in this chapter.**

### 5. If you encounter a special moment of worship between songs, don't get into a hurry to move to the next selection.

It is very important not to break the moments when people are locked into God's presence. This can be a decision time for many people, and for some, their only real connection point with God all week.

### 6. Start and finish strong!

Confidence comes with preparation. Transitions are smooth when each member of your team is familiar with each other and the material. Starting songs, finishing songs, and flow are all mastered when each member of your team strives to perfect his or her skills daily. Musical awareness and spiritual integrity from each worship team/band member will ensure effective transitions.

## Smart Chapter #30
# Musical Transitions
### *Discussion Questions*

1. Do you ever practice making a smooth transition from one song into another while continuing to play, or do you always start and stop every song?

2. What are some things that you can do to help move from one song to another without stopping?

3. While playing a song, if you want to go back and do a chorus again, or if you want to play the chorus of another song in the same key, do you have the freedom and confidence to do this? Try rehearsing this exercise and see how it flows.

## Smart Chapter #31
# Body Language

People come to worship to experience a moment with God. The attitude, body language, and overall presence of the worship team will either enhance this or kill it.

—Spence Smith

The point of practicing how you are communicating through your body language isn't to be overly focused on performance itself, but rather it is to use all of your gifts to the best of your ability to lead others into God's presence.

## 1. Shine.

"Let your light shine before men in such a way that they may see your good works, and glorify your Father who is in heaven" (Matthew 5:16, NASB). Let what you've got inside come out! Move around the stage in a way that captures the emotion of your song. Your body language will say a lot about how you feel about your song. Let your face show that you care about each moment.

## 2. Don't hesitate to play and move with confidence.

If expressing yourself feels awkward, then the following is all the more important. Practice with your delivery and ministry goals in mind. Practice like you play! Athletes train for many hours between events just to remain competitive and sharp. You should approach your leading in the same way. The more practiced and prepared you are, the more capable you are of going where the Spirit wants to lead.

## 3. Make every note count.

Always be reaching for greatness. You rarely see a great musician or artist give a performance that is less than their very best. That is because a great artist knows that each day requires his or her best—in rehearsal as well as performance. That is the road to greatness, the standard of excellence. Your worship team and band should take this same approach. Each day should bring a renewed desire to give God glory by giving your all to the craft!

## 4. Use techniques specific to your instrument to make sections of the song stand out to the audience.

As you perform techniques unique to your instrument, do not hide your instrument from the listeners. Instead, let them see and connect to what you are doing. As part of the band, what you bring to each worship experience is important on so many levels . . . some of which you will never know until heaven. What you play and how you play it onstage may be the moment of ministry for someone in the audience. God has placed in each of us different instruments we connect with— different sounds, tones, and techniques. So play your style and voicings with confidence that God is using everything you offer in worship to bring Him glory! A worshipful, joyful attitude from band members also can impart to a congregation the courage and hunger to go deeper in their relationship with Him. Everything you do is important.

## 5. Be in the moment.

A lot of hard work went into preparing yourself for this worship moment, so really enjoy it, and connect with everything that is happening in the room. Ministry is a powerful thing that changes lives, so take advantage of this opportunity!

## 6. Coaching.

There are a number of reasons we need to connect with our congregation and our listeners. Some of us need more help than others with learning to make that connection, and there's no shame in that. You want to be the best you can be at facilitating a spirit of worship, so do what it takes and make use of every available tool. If you need help, seek out a live producer or coach that can help you with your public speaking and worship presentation.

## 7. Ask, how am I doing?

There is nothing like a friend who will tell you the truth. Often it is hard for us to be objective with ourselves concerning encouragement

**Hot Tip!**

**As an instrumentalist or vocalist and worship team member, try to set up a dress rehearsal for the team and videotape it to see what you look like. Use this to make adjustments to enhance your stage presence.**

or correction. Ask a friend to help evaluate your worship leading skills. Ask him or her what will improve it. Remember, Jesus is your author and your finisher. He loves you and will help you with this process. *And with Him, you can do it!*

**Hot Tip!**

**Courage can only be accessed when you face fear! So, be strong and couragous, and feel God's nearness with you in your time of need.**

## Smart Chapter #31
# Body Language
*Discussion Questions*

1. Are you excited to lead worship and play, or are you terrified and timid? Does it show? If you are excited to lead or play, then let it show! If you are terrified or timid, you need to work on ways to keep it from showing.

2. Do you lead worship with your music, smile, words, and welcoming expressions? What are some things that you can do with your body language to enhance the worship experience?

3. Are you able to stay "in the moment" while leading, or do you worry about what's coming up? What can you do in preparation to allow yourself to better remain "in the moment"?

4. Do you have somebody whom you really trust to evaluate your worship leading/playing? For the artists that might get stage fright from time to time:

Remember that some of the best and most established players, performers, and actors are scared to death. There is a time to deal with what scares you, and there is a time to project confidence even if you are scared. Courage can only be accessed when you face fear! So, be strong and courageous, and feel God's nearness with you in your time of need.

# Endnotes

## Smart Chapter #2

1. Mark Driscoll, speech.
2. Mike Bickle, speech.
3. Charles Spurgeon, "Pray without Ceasing," sermon (no. 1039), delivered March 10, 1872, http://www.spurgeon.org/sermons/1039.htm.

## Smart Chapter #8

4. Tom Jackson, music producer, speech.

# About the Author

*Anthony Skinner* is a commanding singer/songwriter and worship leader who has been developing his craft as a communicator through songs and worship leading for over twenty years. He has led worship or had his songs sung on almost every continent of the globe. Anthony's own worship album *Forever and a Day* and rock album *Crush* have both received acclaim from *Relevant* and *Paste* magazines. He penned "Million Miles," recorded by artist CeCe Winans on her Grammy Award–winning project *Thy Kingdom Come*, and shares a co- writer credit with Chris McClarney on CCLI's top 50, worship song "Love Never Falls." His songs continue to find homes with the likes of the Newsboys, Jesus Culture, Audio Adrenaline, Brian and Jenn Johnson, Chris McClarney, Don Moen, Live Worship from Bethel Church, Laura Story, Trevor Morgan, Brady Toops, New Life Worship, the Daylights, Film, TV, and more. He has also produced worship artists Chris McClarney, Rita Springer, Brady Toops, and Steve Clark.

Anthony's love of music extends beyond the studio and live performance. He finds a profound satisfaction from teaching clinics on songwriting, worship, and finding intimacy with God. He is the president of Orphansake Records and Immersion.tv.

## Additional Contributors

*Ivan Pato* is currently the director of worship at Second Chance Fellowship in Oakland, Florida. He has eighteen years of worship-leading experience with youth and adults. His primary interests and passions all fall within music: writing songs, studio work, giving guitar lessons, and developing relationships with local area worship pastors. Due to this God[given passion, Ivan is always seeking better ways to develop aspiring worship leaders and musicians in the local church and to get them involved in worship ministry.

*Angelo Ballestero* is veteran worship leader and an award-winning songwriter and recording artist. One of his songs, "The Wind Will Carry Me," won first place for songwriting in the Contemporary/Rock category and was overall grand prize winner at the 17th Annual GMA/Christian Artist's Music Seminar in the Rockies, Estes Park, Colorado. Angelo also has experience on the other side of the microphone, having owned and run two recording studios and a full theater and lighting company. He has taught the art of songwriting at Full Sail and conducted various songwriting workshops from Gideon Film Festival to Living Room Worship. He resides in Florida with his wife, author Shelly Ballestero, and their two sons.

Made in the USA
San Bernardino, CA
11 July 2017